# TIMOTHY HEALY:

## MEMORIES AND ANECDOTES.

*Photo*]  [*Werner & Son.*

THE LATE MR. T. M. HEALY, K.C.,
*First Governor-General, I.F.S.*

# TIMOTHY HEALY:
## MEMORIES AND ANECDOTES

### SIR DUNBAR PLUNKET BARTON
BART., P.C., K.C., M.A. (OXON)

HON. D.LITT. OF NATIONAL UNIVERSITY OF IRELAND

## THE TALBOT PRESS LIMITED

### LONDON
## FABER & FABER, LIMITED
24 RUSSELL SQUARE, W.C.1

Printed at
The Talbot Press
DUBLIN

# INTRODUCTION.

THESE chapters form an expansion of a series of articles which were originally communicated by the author to an Irish newspaper. They are republished in their present form at the suggestion of some old friends of Timothy Healy who deplore his loss and retain a vivid recollection of his brilliant and picturesque personality.

Timothy Healy and the author were on different sides in public life. But there were many points of contact between them. They were fellow members of the Irish Bar and of the House of Commons, fellow Benchers of King's Inn in Dublin and of Gray's Inn in London, fellow students of the history, the topography, and the antiquities of Ireland, and comrades in the social side of the legal profession. The author saw a great deal of Timothy Healy, knew him well, and liked him much. It is with sincere respect and affection that he dedicates these pages to the memory of a departed friend.

# CONTENTS

Chapter                                                                      Page

I. The First Phase ... ... ... 11

II. Apprenticeship to Public Life ... ... 19

III. Parliamentary Obstructionist ... ... 27

IV. A Stormy Petrel ... ... ... 35

V. Parliamentary Orator and Debater ... 43

VI. Tiger Tim's Parliamentary Tactics ... 51

VII. Irony and Pathos ... ... ... 59

VIII. Healy's Judgments upon British Statesmen 67

IX. Healy's Judgments upon British Statesmen 75

X. The Irish Bar ... ... ... ... 83

XI. Some Forensic Anecdotes ... ... 91

XII. The Munster Circuit ... ... ... 99

XIII. Gray's Inn ... ... ... ... 107

XIV. The Last Phase ... ... ... 115

Index ... ... ... ... 123

# CHAPTER I.

# THE FIRST PHASE.

# CHAPTER I.

## *The First Phase.*

BANTRY, in West Cork, Timothy Healy's birth-place, is the centre of a district the inhabitants of which are noted for charm and quick-wittedness. An inspector of schools in Ireland once told the author that the young people of West Cork, and of the neighbouring County of Kerry had particularly impressed him by their intellectual brightness and readiness of response.

Timothy Healy's father was the Clerk of the Bantry Poor Law Union. In 1862 he was transferred to a similar post at Lismore in Co. Waterford, which he continued to hold for forty-four years until his death in 1906. Tim, who was seven years old when his family left Bantry, spent the next five years in the river-side town of Lismore, which is situated on the banks of the Blackwater, nestling peacefully under the shadow of the ancient castle of the Dukes of Devonshire.

The families of Cavendish and Healy thus became neighbours, and their relations became and always remained cordial. The Healys were once instrumental in saving the castle from destruction by fire; and a time came, half

a century afterwards, when the Duke of
Devonshire markedly displayed his personal
regard for Tim Healy in all that concerned his
tenure of the office of Governor-General of the
Irish Free State.

I remember the occurrence of an incident at
a trial in Dublin which was illustrative of the
esteem in which Tim Healy's father was held
by those who knew and appreciated his
merits. As Clerk of the Lismore Union he
came to Dublin to give some formal evidence
in his official capacity, and was sitting on a
back bench in the court-house waiting for his
turn to be called to the witness box. The
presiding judge happened to be Chief Baron
Palles, who was the greatest of all the Irish
judges of our time. When the Chief Baron
caught sight of Mr. Healy he invited him to a
seat beside him on the bench. The barristers
in court were curious to know who the stranger
could be to whom the Chief Baron was paying
so marked a compliment, and were interested
when the word passed round that it was the
father of young Timothy Healy, who was then
a rising member of the Bar.

The Healy family was closely allied, both by
friendship and by inter-marriage, with another
West Cork family, the Sullivans. Thus it came
about that Tim Healy married a daughter of
T. D. Sullivan, M.P.; and his brother Maurice
married a daughter of A. M. Sullivan, M.P.

T. D. Sullivan and A. M. Sullivan were brothers. They belonged to the clan of the Sullivans or O'Sullivans which had loomed large through the centuries in the history of Munster. The Sullivans and the Healys were as closely inter-related by political sympathies as they were by family ties. The association of the two families is exemplified at the present day in the Temple, where Mr. Serjeant Sullivan, K.C., a son of A. M. Sullivan, and Maurice Healy, K.C., a nephew of Timothy Healy, pursue their professional avocations as barristers in the same chambers and under the same roof.

At the age of thirteen Tim Healy left Lismore in order to enter a merchant's office in Dublin. He had received his early education at the Christian Brothers' school near his home. Thenceforward he became his own school-master. Among the proficiencies which he acquired with the help of self-education was shorthand-writing. So exceptional was his skill in that useful art that he attracted the notice of Sir Isaac Pitman himself, and became a particular friend and *protégé* of that very famous stenographist.

It was Healy's proficiency in Isaac Pitman's craft that led to his first regular employment, and made him self-supporting while he was still a lad. At the age of sixteen he was appointed shorthand clerk in the office of the

Superintendent of the North-Eastern Railway Company at Newcastle-on-Tyne.

It was a visit to Newcastle of Isaac Butt, K.C., the leader of the Irish National Party of that date, which drew Healy into an active participation in politics. He took a prominent part in the reception of the visitor, and was selected as secretary of the local political organisation which was founded on that occasion.

The personality of Isaac Butt made a deep impression upon young Healy, and exercised a favourable influence upon his subsequent career in more than one direction. I have sometimes heard Healy speak with admiration of the stately eloquence and dignified demeanour which Isaac Butt exhibited both as an advocate and as a senator. Healy did not make him his model in the House of Commons; but, as an advocate, he did not neglect his example. Butt was noted for an attitude of polished and respectful independence towards the Judicial Bench, of which Healy sometimes cited the following illustration.

Butt once defended a client against whom a court had, not without grave provocation, made the mistake of initiating proceedings for contempt of court in the absence of any regular complaint, and on the evidence of a newspaper report. Butt persuaded the court to retreat from this position by the force of an argument from the conclusion of which the following is an extract: " You are grounding here a process," he said, " to destroy a man on a statement behind his back. It violates every principle of British law. Any judgment founded on that evidence will go forth without authority and will return without respect. It will be said of it that it was an indictment without an accuser, a sentence without a trial, and a conviction without evidence. I hope I have not gone beyond my duty in my submission to the court. I know that the surest reverence for authority is often manifested by boldly remonstrating when it is going wrong. If I have been lacking in courtly manners, my defence is—' Be Kent unmannerly when Lear's mad?' " This rhetorical passage was characteristic of the Irish Bar of that era, and was admired by ardent young men like Tim Healy.

Ten years after his meeting with Isaac Butt, Healy was admitted to the Irish Bar. Meanwhile, a door to journalism and to public life was opened to him when he was offered the post of Parliamentary correspondent of the *Nation,* the leading organ of the Irish political movement with which he sympathised. The editor of the *Nation* was A. M. Sullivan, M.P., a very notable Irishman of his time. His son Alexander Martin Sullivan, then a child of seven years of age, is now Mr. Serjeant Sullivan, a leading advocate of the English Bar, and a Bencher of the Middle Temple.

# CHAPTER II.

## APPRENTICESHIP TO PUBLIC LIFE.

# CHAPTER II.

## *Apprenticeship to Public Life.*

### 1878—1880.

In February, 1878, Tim Healy left Newcastle-on-Tyne for London, and started his public career at the age of twenty-three as the parliamentary correspondent of the *Irish Nation*. The young lobbyist thus became, so to speak, a war correspondent at the parliamentary front. His letters to the *Irish Nation* described, with remarkable piquancy and vigour, the active campaign which the Irish members were initiating under a new leader who was taking the place which had formerly been held by Isaac Butt. This was Charles Stewart Parnell. The presence in the Lobbies of the House of Commons of the young parliamentary correspondent of the *Nation,* soon attracted the notice of Parnell, who recognised his tireless energy, his disinterested enthusiasm, his intuitive "sense of the theatre " in Irish politics, his journalistic brilliancy, and his aptitude for organisation.

Parnell in 1879 undertook a mission to raise funds for the Irish cause in America. This adventure in a strange land involved him in a maze of difficulties and perplexities, from which he extricated himself by cabling for the young correspondent of the *Irish Nation* to come to his assistance. Tim Healy responded readily, and became the Irish leader's aide-de-camp during the remainder of his American tour. In this position he proved to be so invaluable to Parnell, that the leader left all the work of organisation and publicity to the young recruit.

Healy's exact relation to Parnell in this episode has been misunderstood by some writers who were not informed of the facts. They regarded him as a paid private secretary of Parnell's. But this idea was entirely erroneous. Whatever post he may have held in the party organisation, he was never in Parnell's personal employment. Parnell was his political chief to whose summons he responded in an emergency.

Healy rendered to Parnell allegiance rather than affection. He was attracted to his chief by his gifts of leadership, by his exceptional force of character, and by his remarkable personality in which so much strength and weakness were blended. One of these weaknesses appears to have been a surprising superstitiousness. Healy, when he became intimate with Parnell, was astonished to find that this strong, silent man of iron will and unwavering purpose was a serious believer in the unluckiness of " thirteen " among numerals, and of " Friday " among the days of the week. Healy has related an incident which happened one night when Parnell was dictating a political document from a sick bed to his secretary. Suddenly the sick man raised himself in the bed and pointed to three candles, by the light of which Healy was writing. Leaning forward he blew out one of them, declaring that he feared that if the document should be written by the light of three candles it might bring disaster to the matter in hand.

In spite of occasional disagreements and of the absence of any temperamental affinity between the two men, Parnell and Healy appear to have worked loyally towards each other until the occurrence of the historic " split " in the Irish Party. They recognised and valued each other's strong points. Healy surrendered himself to Parnell's magnetic leadership; and Parnell trusted Healy's disinterested zeal and utilised his political judgment.

There has been a tendency in some quarters to exaggerate Healy's obligations to Parnell. His introduction to the House of Commons was not the work of Parnell, who was disposed to value him as a secretary and as organiser rather than as an orator or a political leader. In fact, Parnell seems to have shown a disposition to discourage his activities as a public speaker, being of opinion that his usefulness lay in the routine of an office rather than in the centre of an arena. It was not owing to Parnell's patronage, but to an unexpected opportunity which presented itself in Ireland, that Healy picked up, almost by accident, a key to the House of Commons.

Healy's earliest electoral successes flowed directly from the popular *éclat* which he gained by becoming the object of two Crown prosecutions.

The first of these prosecutions was instituted in 1880, shortly after his return from his mission to America. It arose out of an eviction in County Cork, which had a tragic sequel. An evicted tenant in County Cork took refuge with his family under an upturned boat on the sea-shore, where he died from exposure. After his death, his family left their shelter and re-took possession of the farm from which they had been evicted. For doing so they were prosecuted and imprisoned. The distressing circumstances of the case aroused the sympathy of Healy, who made an inflammatory speech in his native town of Bantry, condemning the treatment of the evicted tenant. For this speech he was arrested, and was committed for trial.

Having been released on bail, pending his trial, Healy was presented with a sudden opportunity of becoming a candidate for a vacancy in the parliamentary representation of Wexford, where he was welcomed as a political martyr, and was elected unopposed. His martyrdom had a happy termination, for he soon emerged successfully from his trial at the Cork Assizes. He was defended by Peter O'Brien, afterwards Attorney-General and Lord Chief Justice of Ireland, with the help of whose advocacy he was triumphantly acquitted.

A few years afterwards, in 1883, Healy was again prosecuted, and tried with Michael Davitt for certain violent speeches in the country. On this occasion he was ordered to give securities for good behaviour or suffer imprisonment for six months. He refused to give securities and went to prison. The only thing of which he complained in the six months of his prison life was the " lassitude " which he suffered from " having nothing to do except to read the newspapers." It happened that on the expiry of his sentence a sudden vacancy occurred in the parliamentary representation of the County of Monaghan. The Nationalist party seeing an opportunity of winning the seat for their movement, invited Timothy Healy to become a candidate. He did not hesitate to resign his membership for Wexford, and to jump into the fray. Again his imprisonment served as a passport to the electors. He was triumphantly returned to the House of Commons with the result that his reputation and his influence in Irish politics were considerably enhanced.

There was plenty of variety about his electoral experiences, for he afterwards represented four other constituencies in Parliament— South Londonderry, North Longford, North Louth, and N.E. Cork.

# CHAPTER III.

# PARLIAMENTARY OBSTRUCTIONIST.

# CHAPTER III.

## *Parliamentary Obstructionist.*
### 1880—1885.

DURING his early years in the House of Commons Healy became the *fidus Achates* of Joseph Biggar, who was the vanguard leader in a strenuous campaign of parliamentary obstruction. It was at this period that a prominent Irish Nationalist, John O'Leary, is said to have remarked to Parnell that Timothy Healy seemed to him to have the "*best* head" of all the Irish Nationalist members, and that Parnell is said to have replied, "He has the *only* political head among them." At this stage of his career his head-piece could not have been truly described as an "old head on young shoulders," for he displayed the unmeasured audacity of a youthful political desperado. A time was coming when his parliamentary manners were to become more polished and orderly.

In their obstructionist campaign Joe Biggar and Tim Healy found it necessary to engage in several encounters with successive Speakers of the House, and more than once incurred the extreme penalty of suspension from its sittings. A typical encounter of this kind

occurred in a debate upon a proposal to set
up a new and drastic Standing Order, the
object of which was to give increased powers
of a disciplinary kind to the Speaker. As it
was obvious that this Standing Order was
intended to serve as an effective weapon for
crushing obstructionism, Healy did not hesitate
to let himself go, and to indulge in what an
opponent described as " one of the most
waspish," and an admirer described as " one
of the cleverest and most adroit " attacks ever
made on a person in authority.

Healy began by insinuating that he would
not object to the proposed standing order, if
the increased powers were to be conferred
only upon the present occupant of the Speaker's
Chair, in whose fairness, he mockingly declared,
there was universal confidence; " but," proceeded Healy in the same sarcastic vein, " we
are not permitted to hope that the present
Speaker will always occupy the Chair. And,
if he should cease to do so, what guarantee
have we that he will be succeeded by a gentleman of the same exalted qualities?" He went
on to picture the demerits of some possible
successor of the Speaker in terms which were
obviously intended to convey an ironical
portrait of the Speaker himself. The Speaker
bore this veiled attack until Healy was
emboldened to make a pretence of respectful
candour by admitting that, much as the Irish

members admired the present occupant of the Chair, he would not have been their choice. " No. Their choice would have been a man who excelled even the present Speaker in the qualities essential for the Chair—I allude, of course, to my friend the member for Cavan."

The " member for Cavan " was Joe Biggar himself, the notorious protagonist of parliamentary obstruction. The Speaker's patience was overcome by this sally. " I call," he said in thundering tones, " on the hon. member no longer to pursue this line of argument." Healy assumed a air of embarrassment and confusion, and then fired his parting shot. " I hope," he said, " that the member for Cavan will pardon me for my having compared him, however remotely, with the present occupant of the Speaker's Chair." This turbulent incident enables us to understand Lord Curzon of Kedleston's description of Healy, whom he once described as " the most talented member of the Irish party, with an unsurpassed gift of corrosive humour and almost diabolical irony." When Healy gained more experience he became noticeably respectful towards the authority of the Chair. But this particular duel with the Speaker occurred in his " salad days," when he was sowing his parliamentary wild oats in lavish style.

At this stage of his career Healy once played the part of David in a single combat with a

parliamentary Goliath. The Goliath of this
episode was Sir William Harcourt, a cabinet
minister who towered above his colleagues by
his huge stature and by a domineering
personality which was so powerful as to be
considered by his opponents to be arrogant
and overbearing. In an Irish debate, Healy,
who had to reply to Harcourt, began his speech
as follows: " Mr. Speaker, the speech about
Ireland which we have just listened to from the
Front Bench of the British House of Commons
reminds me of Pope's well-known couplet:
' Where London's column towering to the skies
like a tall bully lifts its head—and lies.' The
House was convulsed in laughter, in which
Harcourt himself could not refrain from joining.

Healy, after several years training and
practice as a pupil of Joe Biggar, succeeded in
carrying the fine art of obstruction to a per-
fection that never has been, and probably never
will be, surpassed. For the purposes of this
fine art, Biggar framed a set of rules which
became the ten commandments of the obstructionist creed. The guiding motives of these rules
were the defiance of all governments, and the
blocking of all government business. One of
the laws in this decalogue was—" Never speak
except in government time." Another was—
" Never resign anything—get expelled." The
rest of them were of an equally peremptory
kind. Healy, having learned these rules by

heart, proceeded to enlarge and amplify them, and to surpass their original inventor in the assiduity and success with which he put them into execution.

Joe Biggar, in spite of an ungainly exterior a rasping voice and an angular manner, had some amiable and attractive qualities which endeared him to Healy. When Biggar died, Healy was deeply touched. He wrote to his brother that it was the greatest blow he had yet received, and in subsequent years he often alluded to Biggar with affection and admiration. For example, on one occasion, when he was a guest at the house of an eminent Irish surgeon, Sir Arthur Chance, the conversation turned upon the character and career of Biggar. Healy remained silent until the host turned to him and said, " When did he die, Mr. Healy?" Tim astonished the company by springing to his feet and exclaiming, " Joe Biggar is not dead. That man can never die. His memory will live in the spirit of the nation for ever!"

# CHAPTER IV.

## A STORMY PETREL.

# CHAPTER IV.

## *A Stormy Petrel.*
### 1885—1891.

No account of Healy's career—however brief or superficial that account may be—would be complete or intelligible without some reference to the part which he took in the crisis which culminated in Parnell's downfall, because it was by this episode that the whole current of his life was diverted into strange channels and became shadowed and embittered.

This is not the place in which to revive the story of the proceedings in the Divorce Court, which resulted in Parnell's downfall. Healy was lying upon a sick-bed in Ireland when the scandal was made public; and he and his friends have always maintained that he took no part in the initiation of the movement for the deposition of " the chief " from the chairmanship of the Irish Party. The truth appears to be that it was not until the " split " had become a *fait accompli* that he, being compelled to make his choice, threw himself into the anti-Parnellite camp. After he had once taken that step, he became one of its fiercest and most relentless spokesmen.

It was in his conflict with Parnell over this

divorce scandal that Healy incurred more odium
and made more enemies than at any other stage
of his life. It cannot be denied that in the
arena of politics, Healy's temperament sometimes led him to strike right and left without
restraint or discrimination, and with a regret-
table disregard of the pain that his blows might
inflict. Almost every man of striking personality
has some defect which is a counterpart of his
better side; and here lay the special defect of
Healy's qualities.

In excuse of Healy's unbridled utterances
about the lady who figured prominently in the
case, it has been urged that he regarded her
as having brought about the ruin of the Irish
cause. Trojan-like he lost his self-restraint in
his references to one who, in his eyes, " like
another Helen had fired another Troy." So far
as the charge of truculence towards Parnell
was concerned, Healy's defence was that
Parnell and his lieutenants had themselves
dropped the buttons from their foils, and that
he was following the French maxim: *A corsair,
corsair et demi.* In justice to Healy it should
be remembered that he often expressed himself
in terms of admiration for Parnell's gifts of
leadership and for his courage in adversity.
For example in his memoirs will be found the
following tribute to Parnell's bearing when he
was defending himself with his back to the
wall: " When rough epithets were hurtling,"

wrote Healy, " we could always—as the French say—discern the gentleman at a league. The old skill, energy, and resourcefulness burned in him. Genius shone like the upcast flame from an expiring candle."

This was not the only instance when Healy, in a calm retrospect, made generous amends for the wounds which he had inflicted in the passionate heat of a political battle. The aftermath of the " Split " in the Nationalist party involved him in frequent collisions with the two Redmonds. Yet, in the memoirs he has done justice to John Redmond's imperturbable good temper and dignity in debate. Of the gallant Willie Redmond he wrote: " When the great war broke out Willie Redmond's soldierly instincts banished the demurs of age. Without the necessity for sacrifice, frank and free, he marched to death with military glee. A fine gentleman, a fast friend, and, at the last, a finished speaker, his soul went out to the thunder of the German guns."

Professor Swift MacNeill relates in his memoirs that there was a time when he had to suffer in debate from Healy's vitriolic attacks, yet he had been deeply touched by his kindness on other occasions, and particularly by his sympathy in a period of trouble and bereavement.

Another countryman with whom Tim Healy came into acute collision was T. P. O'Connor.

Yet a reader of Healy's memoirs will find many appreciative references to " T. P." scattered through its pages. He writes of " T. P." as a " likeable " and " brilliant " fellow-countryman whom he looked upon as the cleverest of all his colleagues. He gave him credit for getting the Irish Labourers Act through the House of Commons, and for many other parliamentary services to Ireland; and he noted with patriotic pride the popularity which " T. P." enjoyed with all parties in the House, and the interest and attention with which the House listened to his speeches.

Healy for a time enjoyed a large measure of political power and influence in Irish journalism and in Irish politics. He took a prominent part in founding a newspaper which ultimately became amalgamated with the journal which was then the principal organ of Irish national-ism. For a time he figured as *par excellence* the stormy petrel of Irish public life, and it looked as if he might have succeeded to Parnell's empty throne. But he was too irreconcilable and uncompromising for such a task as Reunion. He always retained the con-fidence of some of the most enlightened and patriotic of Irishmen. But his political influence in the country waned as time went on, and he gradually became a kind of political Ishmael against whom many hands were raised. Never-theless, he never lost courage or confidence in himself or in the soundness of his own political judgment.

Healy's Irish journalistic experiences in point of adventure and danger can hardly have been rivalled even in Mexico, or in the Wild West. His life was constantly in danger. The windows of his house were smashed. He was held up by gunmen. His newspaper offices were raided, and an attempt was made to blow them up with dynamite. He defended himself from these assaults with weapons of irony. When he was told that a rival newspaper was searching his speeches for materials for their leading articles he replied that he was glad to hear it, because their searches would afford them a liberal education. He added that they badly needed such an education, because their leading articles were " about as interesting as a grocer's circular." They retaliated with a shower of nicknames. For example, one paper called him " a scalp-hunter," and another compared him to " a volcano in constant eruption."

Upon the Irish hustings Healy's sardonic irony and the quickness of his vinegar-tongued repartee gained for him a hearing upon occasions when it otherwise might have been denied. For example, in a Louth election he once accepted a challenge to address a hostile meeting, which was presided over by the redoubtable Mr. A. J. Kettle. The platform was an old-fashioned wagonette, a rickety portion of which gave way, and precipitated the chairman into the crowd.   A shout of " Go down, Kettle; your spout is broken," came from the crowd.   The laughter which rewarded this sally was renewed when Healy ended his speech by politely moving a vote of thanks to Mr. Kettle for "his dignified conduct in the chair."

Healy did not rely on his tongue as his only weapon of defence.   Once, when attacked by a violent rowdy, he is said to have drawn a shillelagh and to have knocked down his assailant.   He never shrank from facing his foes.   To his brother he once wrote, " the hissing of the mob is music in my ear."

# CHAPTER V.

# PARLIAMENTARY ORATOR AND DEBATER.

# CHAPTER V.

## *Parliamentary Orator and Debater.*

AFTER Parnell's downfall there was no commanding figure in the Irish Parliamentary Party to whom Healy could bring himself to render unquestioning obedience. He lacked confidence in the capacity for leadership of any of Parnell's followers, or in their ability to take full advantage of their parliamentary opportunities. Thus he became by degrees more and more independent of party ties, until at last he completely separated himself from the other Irish Nationalist members, and stood out alone as a solitary self-reliant figure, as disinterested as Don Quixote, as piratical as Paul Jones, as sardonic as Dean Swift, and as daring in combat as Prince Rupert.

Healy's independence of discipline, impatience of restraint, and repudiation of the ordinary ties of political allegiance provoked his opponents to tauntingly remind him more than once that he had himself been one of the inventors of the parliamentary pledge which had bound every Nationalist M.P. " to work and vote with the Irish Party." But Healy showed no sign of wincing. His withers were unwrung. Indeed, even his critics could not withhold their admiration of his sang-froid.

43

Sometimes I have seen him holding the House
of Commons by his wit and humour, while
his colleagues watched his success with involuntary admiration. "When I talk," he
wrote, "they don't cheer me. However they
laugh, and I suppose they can't help it."

For several years Healy had a small group
of followers in the House of Commons, but at
last a time came when all his sympathisers
were defeated, and the Healyite Party consisted
of Tim Healy alone. Nevertheless, he resumed
his seat in the House with an air which was
so defiant and so undismayed that a gallery
journalist was moved to sympathise with the
other 83 Irish members, "because," as he put
it, "Mr. Healy had expelled them, and had
turned them all out into the cold."

Healy himself fully realised the humorous
aspect of this situation. One night he sent the
House of Commons into a roar of laughter
when—in response to an appeal for a reunion
of the Irish Party—he declared "There are,
Mr. Speaker, two united Irish Parties in this
House, and I am one of them."

Mr. P. W. Wilson of the *Daily News* and
*Pearson's Magazine* described Healy at this
period as a "strange and solitary enigma." Once
he compared Healy's figure, as he addressed
the House from a corner seat while the other
Irish members watched him from the benches
behind, to that of Napoleon as he appears in

Orchardson's picture of the great Emperor standing in the foreground upon the deck of *Bellerophon* with his marshals grouped in the background. To Mr. Wilson, Healy " looked like Napoleon, with Napoleon's shoulders, bull-neck, corpulence, and habit of holding his well formed, well fleshed hands behind his back as he walked." I confess that, except that both Napoleon and Healy were courageous, and that both walked with their hands behind their backs, this comparison between them is to me more interesting than convincing.

Healy was the readiest of debaters. He never prepared his speeches. " No loss of stray notes would embarrass him," wrote Sir Henry Lucy in *Punch*—" he just talks to the House straight-forth in unpremeditated strain, over the depth of whose pathos and passion flash gleams of mordant wit." His spontaneity and the pictur-esqueness of his appearance and style operated like passports to both the ear and the eye, and the House used to fill rapidly whenever it became known that Tim Healy was " up."

" Healy's parliamentary gifts," wrote Lord Birkenhead, " were individual and extraordi-nary. He possessed a power of mordant and corrosive sarcasm, the like of which I have never met elsewhere. I can still see him standing up to address the House, his chin aggressively protruded, his expression one of melancholy gravity, pouring out a long succession of bitter and wounding insults. His wit was as extraordinary as his invective. He possessed also another quality not less effective in his oratorical stock-in-trade. He was amazingly arresting as a speaker. When Healy was speaking you had to listen to him all the time, whether you wanted to or not. Had Edmund Burke added this quality to his expert intellectual equipment, we should, perhaps, not have lost the American colonies."

Healy was gifted with a natural capacity for lighting up a political situation with some apt quotation, some humorous analogy, or some witty flash. For example, when a dying government was carrying on a precarious existence from day to day he compared them to " the hunted hind, oft doomed to death, yet fated not to die." When an invitation was conveyed to him by an Irish Viceroy to an interview which might have compromised him politically, he declined it, and excused himself for doing so by observing that the Viceroy's invitation made him " feel like a lady who was being woo'd without the prospect of lawful espousals." He once invited the President of the Board of Agriculture, Mr. Runciman, whose appearance was more dapper than rustic, to inform himself about some of the departmental duties by visiting an Irish fair " disguised as an agriculturist." He once described an eloquent fellow countryman who had much wit and

popularity, but was rather short in height, as
" a duodecimo Demosthenes."

When that popular highlander, Sir Henry
Campbell-Bannerman, was appointed Chief
Secretary for Ireland, Healy congratulated the
Prime Minister upon his " happy idea of governing Ireland through a mist of Scotch jokes."
When a Chief Secretary for Ireland happened
to be temporarily indisposed, Healy described
an Irish Bill to which he was opposed as " the
offspring of a sick headache at the Irish Office."
After one of Healy's antagonists, Tom Quinn
by name, had caused a defeat of his party by
falling asleep in a lobby and missing a division,
Tim Healy greeted his next re-appearance in
the House with a couplet:

> " Let Ireland shout, let England quake,
>   Tom Quinn's awake, Tom Quinn's awake."

Such was Healy in Parliament. He was by
turns witty, pathetic or mordant. But, whatever mood he was in, he never failed to enchain
the attention of the House. If I were asked to
name the personal traits which enchained a
listener's attention to whatever Healy said, I
think I should reply that they were his low
modulated voice which lent itself equally well
to the note of humour and of pathos, and the
almost supernatural gravity with which he
could emit the most laughter-provoking *bon
mots*.

# CHAPTER VI.

# TIGER TIM'S PARLIAMENTARY TACTICS.

# CHAPTER VI.

## Tiger Tim's Parliamentary Tactics.

THERE was a Jekyll-Hyde duality in Tim Healy's parliamentary activities and reputation. To the House of Commons he was personally acceptable, and to his friends he was always a gentle and lovable companion. But so predatory and so cunning was the way in which he prowled at large in the devious depths of the parliamentary jungle, so quick was his " wildcat spring," and so vitriolic was his vocabulary that a journalist in the Press Gallery of the House christened him " Tiger Tim," and the illustrated papers were fond of portraying him as a ferocious quadruped with a striped body, a feline poise and a carnivorous expression in his eyes.

Advancing age never seemed to weaken the irrepressible effervescence of Healy's activities. He never ceased to be a " buoyant boy." Somebody described him, after he had long passed his meridian, as "a *gamin* but a *gamin* of genius." In a similar sense it was said of him that to the end of his political career he never lost " an air of impish juvenility." He remained a sort of parliamentary " Peter Pan," who never grew old.

Healy was the inventor of a parliamentary device which became known to the initiated as " The Collusive Block." When he anticipated that a desirable measure was in danger of being blocked, he adopted the bold device of blocking it in the names of himself and of several trusted associates. He defended himself from criticism for resorting to such ingenious devices by pleading that he was " counteracting obstruction " by throwing dust in the eyes of his adversaries. The Collusive Block cleared the paths of several Irish Bills to the Statute Book. Their opponents supposing that the Bill had been effectually obstructed, neglected to block it themselves. When the time had passed for serving any fresh blocking notices Healy withdrew his bogus blocks. As a result of these manœuvres, the measure became unopposed and passed into law by means of Healy's skilful use of " The Collusive Block."

It must not be supposed that Tim Healy's work as a parliamentary debater and a tactician was merely destructive. He also employed his debating skill and his intimate knowledge of parliamentary practice very successfully in the active field of constructive legislation. A notable example was the so-called " Healy Clause " in the Irish Land Act of 1881, protecting a tenant's improvements from the imposition of rent, which he drafted and piloted through several stormy debates.

This clause was saved from shipwreck by a simple and daring subterfuge of Healy's. The Government, in the interests of parliamentary time, came to the conclusion, on the Report stage, that either this highly contentious clause must be abandoned, or the whole Bill must be withdrawn. When Healy heard that his favourite clause was in danger he went to the Government and suggested that, if the clause were transferred from the end of the Bill to the beginning, its opponents might be taken by surprise, and the Bill with the clause in it might slip through. Arthur Balfour objected that such a transfer of a clause from one part of a Bill to another could not be done without leave of the House. " Oh no," said Healy, " the printers will do it if you ask them." " I never knew that," said Balfour. " Try it," said Healy. It was tried successfully with the result that the Bill, including the " Healy Clause," passed the Report stage without difficulty.

A life-like pen-portrait of Healy in the character of a parliamentary tactician was painted by Lord Beaverbrook in the *Sunday Express,* where he broached the question "Who was the greatest parliamentarian of my time?" " If," he wrote, " the term is used in its widest possible sense, it would be a complex task to give a correct answer. But if ' parliamentarian ' means the greatest master of the forms of

Parliament, the greatest artist in getting things
to happen there in the way he wanted, then I
would always answer unhesitatingly, 'Tim
Healy.' He knew not only every form of the
House, and every trick in the game, but he also
knew humanity, and he could play on the
House as a musician would play on the organ—
just putting in or taking out the stops while
the instrument responded."

Healy and Lord Beaverbrook were intimate
friends, and Healy once found an opportunity
of coming to his friend's rescue. When Lord
Beaverbrook was Minister of Public Information
he became the object of a factious onslaught
which was utterly routed by the tactical inter-
vention of Tim Healy, who adroitly managed
to turn the whole debate into another channel.
The Minister for Information ceased to be the
object of pursuit. The huntsmen and the
hounds had all galloped away on the track of
Healy's red herring. It was this incident which
moved Lord Beaverbrook to call Tim Healy
" the master of red-herring tactics."

Healy's dexterity in utilising parliamentary
forms for his own purpose, and in turning
debates into unexpected channels won him
several other nicknames beside the one which
Lord Beaverbrook gave him of the " master
of red-herring tactics." For example, it was
the historian Lecky who dubbed him a " master
of two-o'clock-in-the-morning tactics." It

appeared that on the occasion of a late sitting
a measure in which Lecky was interested was
defeated for the simple reason that Healy was
wide-awake and caught the historian napping.
Some of his nicknames gave him credit for
daring as well as for cunning. For example,
a Pressman in the gallery once described Healy
as the " beau-ideal of a buccaneer in broadcloth."

# CHAPTER VII.

## IRONY AND PATHOS.

# CHAPTER VII.

## *Irony and Pathos.*

Of all Healy's parliamentary performances the one which is best remembered by those who heard it, and is most frequently cited as an example of his readiness and versatility, was his speech about " Uganda."

In October, 1902, the Prime Minister, Mr. Arthur Balfour, moved that " for the remainder of the session Government business shall have precedence over all other public and private business." In introducing his motion the Prime Minister mentioned that the question of the making of a railway in Uganda was one of the items of Government business which must be disposed of before the end of the session. It followed, as a result of this motion, that the making of this railway in Uganda was to be given precedence over a vast amount of other public and private business which included several Irish measures which the Irish members regarded as important and urgent. Ireland was in a disturbed and discontented condition, and the Irish members were unanimously opposed to the motion. The Speaker sternly ruled their protests to be out of order, because Government business included

no measure relating to Ireland. For the
moment they were silenced.

Suddenly Tim Healy rose from his seat, and
completely circumvented the Speaker's ruling
by assuming for the moment the character of
a " native of Uganda," and so making his speech
relevant to the Prime Minister's motion. As a
" native of Uganda " he thanked the Government for the interest which they were taking in
his country, which he humorously referred to
as " a distant and neglected island." " As a
native of Uganda," he expressed his gratitude
for the millions of public money which it was
proposed to spend upon " the niggers, the
painted savages, and the heathen," who were
" roaming at large in the forests of Uganda."
" As a native of Uganda," he assured the
Government that when the news of their bounty
reached other parts of the Empire, it would
bring " joy to Canada, good cheer to Australia,
calm to Kerry, and balm to Ballydehob," and
he wound up with a peroration in which he
declared that the Irish members would return
to their country, " elevated and ennobled by
the reflection, that, although Ireland was palpi-
tating with passion, although Connaught was
desolate and although Munster was plunged in
misery, the House of Commons at least had a
watchful care for the people of his native
Uganda." A London paper shortly afterwards
in criticising the Irish members from a hostile

point of view, nick-named them the " Hibernian Comedy Company," but added that " if they produced such admirable performers as Mr. Healy all the time, the House could endure the pain."

Healy had many moods. He could be sardonic, mordant and ironical. But he could also be moving and pathetic, and, when he was in this mood, his style became singularly simple in thought and language. His eyes assumed a drowsy look, and he seemed to speak with a flood of tears in a low modulated voice. A good example was a speech which he delivered upon Mr. Balfour's Education Bill, in defence of religious education in Catholic schools. His concluding words were to the following effect:

" I would rather have my children learn to say ' Our Father ' than learn the use of the Globes. I would rather that they understood their religion so as to prepare them for the eternity that is to come than they should become rich and prosperous, and educated in the things of this world. I think there are more precious things than what is commonly called education. I cannot spell myself. I cannot parse an English sentence. I cannot do the rule of three. I am supposed to know a little law, but I think that is a mistake. But if there is one thing which I and mine have got a grip of, it is the belief in the infinite Christ to come,

and the conviction that our children, whatever
be their distress, whatever be their misfortunes,
whatever be their poverty in this world, if they
have listened to the teaching of the Church,
will reap a rich reward in putting into practice
the lessons of Christianity which they receive
in the Catholic schools."

These simple words, spoken in an audible
whisper, with a tone of deep sincerity and in
a spirit of Celtic enthusiasm and religious
inspiration created a profound impression upon
the House. A discordant note was struck when
a matter-of-fact educationalist got up and
taunted Healy with his admission that he could
not spell, but the questioner seemed to be dis-
armed when Healy blandly asked, " Who can?"

Healy's parliamentary career was a singularly disinterested one. He looked for no
rewards, and until the conclusion of a Treaty
had accomplished what he regarded as a settlement of the old quarrel with England, he
would accept no office.

There was one occasion upon which Healy
accepted a public gift from America. In 1893
a scuffle occurred in the House of Commons
which caused much excitement and com-
ment in America, where it was reported
in the newspapers that Healy's hat had
been smashed in the parliamentary mêlée.
Next day he received a telegram from the
Mayor and Corporation of the city of Alex-

andria, in Louisiana, informing him that the
City Fathers had voted him a silk hat to
replace the battered one. In due course the
silk hat arrived, and Healy wore it on
suitable occasions for twenty-five years until
he resigned his seat in Parliament in 1918. He
must have brushed and ironed it with great
care, because it retained its gloss to the end.
Many a time and oft did he doff it to the
Speaker, and it served as his helmet in more
than one hard-fought encounter.

It was in 1918 that Healy made his final
appearance in the House of Commons, where
he had played a conspicuous part for so many
years. The resignation of his seat in Parliament
was tendered as a protest against certain con-
victions and heavy punishments awarded by
courts martial for offences which he considered
to be trivial. He declared that these proceedings " made his blood boil." He also had
larger reasons for wishing to withdraw from
Parliament. He had come to the conclusion
that the Irish problem had ceased to admit of
a parliamentary solution, and he had made up
his mind " to shake the dust of Westminster
off his feet."

# CHAPTER VIII.

## HEALY'S JUDGMENTS UPON BRITISH STATESMEN.

# CHAPTER VIII.

*Healy's Judgments upon British Statesmen.*

TIMOTHY HEALY was singularly frank and un-
biassed in his judgment of public men, and he
frequently indulged in vivid sketches of his
contemporaries and in witty *bon mots* about
them.

The criterion by which Healy was naturally
disposed to judge British statesmen was their
attitude towards Ireland. Tried by this touch-
stone, Gladstone always held the first place in
his estimation. " The services Gladstone
rendered to Ireland," he once wrote " were
immeasurable. Gratitude cannot repay him:
To blazon his achievements in converting world
opinion would need the harnessing of a lightning flash."

Gladstone reciprocated the interest which
Healy took in him. When the Irish Land Act
was under discussion, Mr. Gladstone used to
say that there were only three men in the House
who understood the principles and detail of
the Act—the Irish Attorney-General, Timothy
Healy, and himself. The " Grand Old Man "
sought the society of the brilliant young man,
and invited him to be his guest both at his
country seat at Hawarden, and at the Prime

Minister's official residence in Downing Street.
Tim Healy declined the invitation to Hawarden,
but he dined occasionally with the Prime
Minister at Downing Street. " I will take no
refusal," the " Old Man " would say. " He
had a winning way with him," said Healy, " and
I yielded, though feeling shy."

The " Old Lion " and the " Tiger Cub " were
capable of drawing each other out, with the
result that they had some interesting conver-
sations. For example, Healy once expressed
the opinion that the Turks were a religious
people, although mistaken in their beliefs, and
cited, as evidence, their daily prayers to Allah
from the minarets at noon. Gladstone's answer
was, " I got one of them to ascend and pray
at 10 o'clock for five piastres."

When Gladstone disappeared from the
political stage Healy was profoundly dissatisfied
with his successors, among whom John Morley,
Lloyd George, and Lord Rosebery were
prominent. Their attitude towards Ireland
seemed to Healy to compare with those of the
" Grand Old Man " " as water compared with
wine." He once said that generosity towards
Ireland was buried with Gladstone in Westminster Abbey.

He entertained a personal regard and respect
for John Morley, but considered him to be
lacking in the fortitude which was requisite for
great purposes. Once he referred to him as the

' Grand Old Maid," and remarked that " his stamina was measurable by his resignation of office when war was declared in 1914."

When Morley became Chief Secretary for Ireland Healy held aloof from him, and abstained from calling at his official lodge in Phoenix Park. Morley took up his pen and protested against this unexpected boycott. In doing so he reminded Healy that " Cato and Brutus were admirable public characters, but they lived a long time ago, and their methods were out of date." Healy in his reply reciprocated Morley's friendly sentiments. " I was sick and you visited me," he wrote, " and so far as non-political elements are concerned they are all on your side. But it is precisely because of this and because personal relations of a friendly kind tend to blunt or destroy the power or the will to criticise that I conceive that for the present it is our duty to hold aloof."

Some Irish members when asked how the new Chief Secretary (John Morley) should be treated, replied: " Treat him like an ass at a fair; leave him alone until he goes astray." This piece of pungent advice had something so Healyesque about it that it was commonly attributed to Tiger Tim, who, however, very definitely denied the imputation.

Lloyd George's fire and combativeness appealed to Healy, who regarded him as " a broth of a boy." But he disliked Lloyd George's

Nonconformist prejudices, and he ridiculed his
aggressive radicalism in the following parody
of Lord John Manners' famous tag:

" Let wealth and commerce, laws and learning
    die,
   But leave us still our new democracy."

On the other hand, he appreciated the Welsh
leader's good humour. Many a skirmish was
fought between the " Irish Tiger " and the
" Welsh Wizard "; and at the end of them all
Healy observed: " After none of my tourneys
could I discern rancour below skin-depth in
that buoyant Celt."

Lord Rosebery's attitude on the Irish question
disappointed Healy, who once is reported to
have said of him: " The noble lord is the kind
of man with whom I should be willing to go
tiger-hunting in the Zoo but not in the jungle."
He liked Birrell and relished his " Birrellisms."
He considered him to be a delightful and ready
speaker. "Besides," he added modestly, " unlike
me he is a scholar."

Tim Healy enjoyed " big-game hunting," and
took particular pleasure in stalking Joseph
Chamberlain, who was the biggest of all the
" big game " to be found in the parliamentary
game preserves of that time.  On one occasion,
when Mr. Parnell was away from the House,
Joseph Chamberlain twitted the Irish members
with indulging in extravagant antics in the

absence of their leader. " When the cat's away the mice play," said Chamberlain. " And what about the rats?" cried Healy, who regarded Joseph Chamberlain and his party as deserters from the Irish cause.

On another occasion, during the South African war, Mr. Chamberlain was being heckled in the House of Commons by questions which were intended to suggest that there had been a great deal of stupidity and blundering in the transportation and organisation of troops, supplies, and materials. The Minister met these suggestions by telling the House how many men had been sent out, how many guns, and finally how many horses. At the mention of horses Healy intervened and convulsed the House by asking: " Can the right hon. gentleman say how many asses have been sent out?"

Once, and once only, Healy was moved to intervene in a manner that was helpful to Chamberlain. In a South African debate a section of the House took up a somewhat self-complacent and sanctimonious attitude by representing that they "washed their hands of" the South African war, and that, so to speak, they were innocent of the blood of these righteous men. When they vehemently applauded an onslaught of Healy's against Chamberlain, Tim, who disliked their air of pretentious self-satisfaction, turned upon them contemptuously and said: " Honourable members opposite applaud and say ' hear, hear '; but I cannot see what credit they can claim for these transactions. They have done nothing except sit in a row upon those benches washing their hands like a band of petty Pontius Pilates."

# CHAPTER IX.

## HEALY'S JUDGMENTS UPON BRITISH STATESMEN.

### (Continued.)

# CHAPTER IX.

*Healy's Judgments upon British Statesmen.*
*(Continued.)*

ONE of the points of difference between Tim
Healy and his Irish colleagues was a divergence
in their respective attitudes towards the two
English parties. His motto in the parliamentary
battlefields was " a plague in both your houses."
But he was always prepared to accept benefits
for Ireland from any quarter, and, when the
Conservatives were in power, he encouraged
them to undertake measures of Irish reform.
He declared more than once that, " after the
retirement of Mr. Gladstone the only remedial
measures for Ireland not yielded to crime were
those of Arthur Balfour, Gerald Balfour, and
George Wyndham."

It became Arthur Balfour's duty at one stage
of his career to incur bitter opposition from the
Irish Nationalist party. Nevertheless, Healy
paid him more than one tribute of personal
appreciation, and once described him as the
" most remarkable of all the Chief Secretaries
of Ireland."

To Gerald Balfour Healy was particularly
grateful for having steered several measures of
Irish Reform through the House of Commons.

The principal of these were the Irish Land
Act of 1896, and the Irish Local Government
Act of 1898, towards the passage of both of
which Tim Healy rendered him valuable assistance. *Punch* hit off this episode in a cartoon
of the hunting field. Healy was depicted
in Irish costume approaching a formidable
fence, mounted on a donkey, followed by the
Irish Chief Secretary, to whom he was shout-
ing: " Come along, Mr. Gerald. I'll make it
aisy for yez."

Next to Gladstone, the second name on
Healy's list of great Englishmen was George
Wyndham, whom he once described as a
" child of genius." " No soul more accordant
with Ireland than Wyndham," he once wrote,
" ever came out of England." George Wyndham
had inherited genuine enthusiasm for
Ireland from his great-grandfather, Lord
Edward Fitzgerald, who was the most romantic
figure in the Irish Rebellion of 1798. It was
characteristic of Wyndham that the first thing
he did after landing on Irish soil as Chief
Secretary was to find his way to the vault
of a church in Dublin where Lord Edward
Fitzgerald's body still lies. Healy was touched
by this incident. He was also deeply affected
when George Wyndham's wife, Lady
Grosvenor, showed him with mingled pride
and emotion some personal relics of Lord
Edward.

Healy was grateful to Wyndham for the passage of Wyndham's Land Purchase Act, which Healy regarded as a charter of the Irish Tenants' liberties. He also admired the character of the man. " George Wyndham's mind," he wrote, " was animated by a soul of the rarest and noblest order." Wyndham reciprocated Healy's friendship. It was he who gave the name of " Heliopolis " to Healy's country house. Some years afterwards the Viceregal Lodge was nicknamed " Uncle Tim's Cabin," when Healy occupied it as Governor-General.

Tim Healy's first glimpse of Lord Birkenhead was on the occasion of the brilliant maiden speech with which young F. E. Smith electrified the House of Commons in 1906. Tim was astonished. Here was a new star in the parliamentary firmament, and he was not slow to recognise that it was a star of the first magnitude.

" F. E.," after his successful speech, had to leave the House hurriedly in order to catch the night mail for Liverpool, where he had to appear in court next morning. As he passed through the lobby a messenger put the following note into his hand: " I am an old man, and you are a young man—yet you have beaten me at my own game.—Tim Healy." Lord Birkenhead often alluded in conversation to this " little crumpled note," and to the

encouragement which he derived from it.
*Apropos* of the pleasure which this note gave
him, " F. E." quoted Dr. Johnson's remark
about an appreciative friend. " I like the
fellow," said Dr. Johnson, " because he flatters
me." " F. E." was also fond of recalling another
crumpled note which he received from Healy
on another occasion. These were " F. E.'s"
own words:

" I recall an occasion," wrote Lord Birkenhead, " when a book on the South African war
was made the subject of a libel action by a
non-commissioned officer, whom it charged
with cowardice. Healy was counsel for the
plaintiff, and I was counsel for the author of
the book. In my closing speech for the defence
I made a contrast between the gallantry of the
British Army generally and that of the soldier
who was Mr. Healy's client, closing with the
lines:

> ' On Fame's eternal camping ground
> Their silent tents are spread;
> And Glory guards with solemn round
> The bivouac of the Dead.'

" After this speech I received a pencilled
note from Tim Healy: ' I did not think that
anybody in England knew these lines except
myself. Who wrote them?' I happened to
know the writer's name, and was able to

whisper across the court to Healy the words,
' Theodore O'Hara, of New York.' "

Many other instances might be given where
Tim Healy, with all his intensity of political
passion and all his vehemence of invective
showed that he was " not blind " to the best
traits of his opponents.  He had unmeasured
affection and admiration for Sir Henry Duke,[1]
who became Chief Secretary for Ireland, and
President of the Probate Divorce and Admiralty
Court under the title of Lord Merrivale.  He
represented Healy's ideal of English fairness
of mind and of English dignity of character.

With Sir Edward Carson[2] he had many a
strenuous combat both in Parliament and in
the political trials, in which Carson prosecuted
and Healy defended; but there was no ill-will
on either side.  He once bearded Edward
Carson in his den, and endeavoured to get some
concession from him.  When asked the result
of his interview, he replied: " I found Carson
the same friendly fellow he has always been,
but he would not budge an inch."

Healy used to be in chronic collision with a
succession of Chief Secretaries, among whom
were Sir Michael Hicks-Beach[3] and Walter
Long;[4] yet in candid moments he was heard to

1 Afterwards Lord Merrivale.
2 Afterwards Lord Carson.
3 Viscount St. Aldwyn.
4 Afterwards Viscount Long of Wraxall.

say of Hicks-Beach that his " icy exterior covered an honest heart," and of Walter Long that he was a " broadminded and fairminded fellow incapable of acting dishonestly towards a political opponent." Of Chief Justice O'Brien, whom some of Healy's colleagues attacked bitterly and nicknamed " Peter the Packer," Healy once said, " Although Peter O'Brien is regarded by some of us as a monster, I know very well that he is  surcharged with human traits."

# CHAPTER X.

## THE IRISH BAR.

# CHAPTER X.

## The Irish Bar.

LET us turn to Tim Healy's career at the Bar, about which I can write with the aid of many vivid personal reminiscences. For many years we were fellow barristers, and afterwards we were fellow Benchers of King's Inn in Dublin, and of Gray's Inn in London. We sat in Parliament on opposite benches for eight years. Having watched him with interest in both arenas I can testify that he displayed at the Bar many of the qualities which distinguished him in Parliament. His speeches at the Bar were sprinkled with plenty of effective and picturesque metaphors, which he drew—sometimes from his storehouse of study and self-education, sometimes from his vivid imagination and ready wit, and sometimes from his happy knack of illustrating the matter in hand by an allusion to some popular or familiar topic, for example, to the rules and devices of the prize ring, the racecourse or the Stock Exchange. He studied the traditional tactics of advocacy; and he took pains to adapt his style and methods to the psychology of judges and jurors. It was one of his maxims that " adroitness and a knowledge of the tribunal counts in advocacy more than any mastery of the law."

Healy's frank estimate of his own standing at the Bar is disclosed in the following intimate letter written to his father at a time at which he was the object of a great deal of vehement political animosity. " I do some work better than others," he wrote, " but in another set I am no good. Yet, in my own line I will earn a living always, despite malice and all uncharitableness. Every professional man is kind to me, young and old." This simple passage in an intimate letter is very characteristic of the marked modesty and candour which were never absent from the writer's mind. He was entirely free from personal vanity or pretentiousness.

Healy's strongest point as a lawyer was an unrivalled familiarity with the Irish Statute law of his own time. This branch of legal knowledge—which comprised the Irish Land Acts, Local Government Acts, Licensing Acts and Labourers Acts—represented a large part of the everyday practice of an Irish lawyer; and nobody at the Irish Bar was better versed in these groups of statutes than Tim Healy. He and his brother, Maurice, had been prominent in the House of Commons among their principal architects, and Tim was at home with their complicated ramifications.

Healy rarely indulged in " gestures," but

there was a curious involuntary movement of his right arm which sometimes heralded a joke. I remember a colleague whispering to me while Healy was speaking: " If you watch him you can tell beforehand when he is going to say something funny. He will stand with his hands behind his back until something funny is coming along. Then he will shoot his right hand out, and will stroke the back of his head twice. At the second stroke the joke will drop out automatically." My friend turned out to be right. I watched and waited; and, sure enough, whenever the time came for him to say something humorous, the right hand which was folded behind his back made a rapid upward movement and began to stroke the back of his head. After the second stroke a humorous observation dropped from his mouth with clock-like regularity.

Although Healy rarely indulged in gesture he sometimes reinforced an argument with melodramatic demonstrativeness. On one occasion he was defending an action for the pollution of a stream. He was counsel for the defendant, whose case was that the stream was absolutely pure and undefiled. In his speech Tim suddenly startled the court by saying: " They say the water is polluted. My lord, look at it. There is a sample." He then drew a bottle from his pocket, uncorked it, and drank it, adding, with great solemnity, " the first drink of water I have had for many a year."

Tim Healy once figured in the Law Courts not as an advocate, but as a plaintiff in a libel action which caused a sensation in its day. After Parnell's downfall he became the object of a fierce campaign of defamation in the Irish press and upon Irish platforms. He waited until a specific charge was formulated, and then promptly issued a writ for libel. The charge was that in a criminal case he had failed in his professional duty in advising his clients to plead guilty. The charge was, of course, utterly unfounded. Healy's action for libel was tried at Limerick, where the jury found that the charge was false, but disagreed as to damages. Ultimately, the question of damages was left to the arbitration of Sir Samuel Walker, an ex-Lord Chancellor of Ireland, who awarded Healy £700.

I remember with what sympathy and good-will towards Healy the legal profession followed the course of these proceedings. Indeed, it is not too much to say that Tim Healy was universally liked and trusted by the legal profession and by the judiciary. He was a fearless advocate, and he was noted for courtesy and good faith in all his relations with both the Bar and the Bench. The Bar and the Bench cordially reciprocated his attitude towards them, and he knew it, for he has written in his memoirs: " I have received nothing but kindness from the members of my profession, gentle and simple, for twenty years."

Healy was one of the few lawyers of the time who wore the silk gown of a King's Counsel both in Ireland and England. In Ireland Healy was " offered silk," as the saying is, by the Irish Lord Chancellor, Lord Ashbourne, in 1899, after he had been fifteen years at the Irish Bar. He had not asked for it, directly or indirectly; and Lord Ashbourne pointed out that it placed him under no obligation because it was a recognition of his professional status. He accepted the offer, and thus became a King's Counsel of Ireland.

Eleven years afterwards he met the Lord Chancellor of Great Britain, Lord Loreburn, in the corridors of the House of Commons. " Can I do anything for you, Healy?" said the Lord Chancellor, who, as Sir Robert Reid, had known him well in Parliament. " Well," said Healy, with a twinkle in his eye, " are there any Bishoprics vacant?" " No," said the Lord Chancellor, laughingly. " Then," said Healy, " since you cannot give me ' lawn ' you might give me ' silk.' " The Lord Chancellor smiled a willing assent, and Healy thus became a King's Counsel in England as well as in Ireland.

# CHAPTER XI.

## SOME FORENSIC ANECDOTES.

# CHAPTER XI.

## Some Forensic Anecdotes.

TIM HEALY was noted at the Irish Bar for his witty sallies. Sometimes they sprinkled and irradiated his speeches, sometimes they enlivened his cross-examination, sometimes they flashed in witty answers to questions from the Bench.

He was particularly happy in an interchange of *bon mots* with Baron Dowse, who was a famous wit of his time. Healy's wit struck on Dowse's like a match on a matchbox. Healy used to tell the story of a ready reply which Dowse, when Solicitor-General for Ireland, gave to another parliamentary wit named Bernal Osborne, who, having made a serious accusation against Dowse, had found that he had been mistaken, and was driven to admit himself to be in the wrong. " I find, Mr. Speaker," he said, " that I must withdraw what I said against the Irish Solicitor-General." Dowse at once rose and said, " Mr. Speaker, as the right honourable gentleman has found it necessary to withdraw what he has said against me, I have much pleasure in withdrawing what I was going to say against him."

On one occasion when Healy was arguing a

case before Baron Dowse, the judge interrupted
him with the question, " Do you go to sleep
with your books, Mr. Healy?" " No, my lord,"
replied Tim, " for Blackstone declares that the
law is a lady that loveth to lie alone."

Dowse was not the only judge who enjoyed
drawing Healy out, as the following story will
show. It was customary in the Irish courts
when a list of motions was being disposed of to
have the list called twice. When a barrister or
solicitor was not ready to move his motion at
the first calling he used to say "Second Calling."
The motion was then passed over and dealt
with on the second calling of the list. Professional men were expected to be ready at
the first calling, and any unreasonable or
habitual negligence on their part in this respect
was noticed and discouraged. This familiar
practice was the occasion of a witty reply which
Tim Healy once made to Lord Chief Justice
O'Brien in the course of the arguments in a
case in which it became material to discuss
certain accusations of negligence which had
been made against a solicitor. The Lord Chief
Justice put the following question to Tim
Healy, who was one of the Counsel in the case:
" What kind of a man, Mr. Healy, would you
say this solicitor was? " Healy replied
promptly: " The kind of man, my lord, who,
when the last trumpet sounds, will wake up
and mutter ' Second Calling.' "

In another case Tim was appearing for the defendant in a Chancery action in which a landowner sought an injunction against some turbulent neighbour for cutting down and carrying away his timber. A young forester gave evidence for the plaintiff. Healy's cross-examination was short and amusing. " How old are you?" asked Tim. " Only twenty-two," said the forester. "And how long have you been a forester?" "Only two years," said the witness. Tim sat down, remarking to the judge, " A regular babe in the wood, my lord."

Healy appeared as counsel in a case in which some scientific question of a technical kind was in issue before Sir John Ross, an eminent judge who was afterwards the last of the Lord Chancellors of Ireland. The judge, in the course of the hearing of the case, expressed his regret that in the trial of so technical a case, he was without the help of an expert adviser, and remarked that in the Admiralty Court the judge always had the aid of a nautical assessor. " Yes, my lord," said Healy, " but in the Admiralty Court the judge is ' at sea,' which your lordship never is."

One of Tim Healy's principal antagonists at the Irish Bar was James Campbell, afterwards Lord Glenavy, Lord Chancellor of Ireland under the old regime, and afterwards President of the Senate of the Irish Free State. Healy and

Campbell differed so widely in temperament
and method that they served as foils to set off
each others distinctive qualities. Campbell used
to banter Healy when he gave way to Celtic
pathos and emotionalism, and Healy used to
retaliate by twitting Campbell for excessive
flintiness of heart. One of their forensic duels
has become famous. I shall tell it as it was
told to me. On one occasion Campbell was
so carried away by the wrongs of a client as
to astonish everybody in court by shedding
tears. Healy, in addressing the jury, declared
that he was glad to have lived to see such a
phenomenon. " It was," he added, " the most
miraculous flow of water since Moses struck
the rock." [a]

Tim Healy once appeared for the defendant
in an action for breach of promise which had
been brought by a lady who had seen seventy-
five summers against a gentleman who was
verging upon ninety-five. In order to counterfeit
juvenility, the lady entered the witness-box clad
in girlish costume, while her features were
swathed in yards and yards of muslin, which
she wore as a veil attached to a very large
picture hat. In her examination-in-chief her
sobbing voice could be faintly heard from
behind these gauzy clouds. At last Tim stood
up to cross-examine her. " Madam," said he,

[a] Another version of the story is that Healy exclaimed, " The
greatest miracle since Moses struck the rock !"

" will you remove the yashmak?" " I do not understand you, sir," she said. " Will you dis-cocoon yourself, madam?" said he. The plaintiff's case from that moment gradually died away in laughter.

# CHAPTER XII.

# THE MUNSTER CIRCUIT.

# CHAPTER XII.

## *The Munster Circuit.*

THE Munster Circuit, of which Tim Healy was a member, was celebrated for the wit of its members, and for the mirth and hilarity of its social life. When Healy became a member of of the circuit its leaders included John Atkinson, afterwards Lord Atkinson, and Peter O'Brien, who afterwards became Lord O'Brien of Kilfenora, and Lord Chief Justice of Ireland. The most nimble-witted of them all, in droll fancy and witty word-play, was Richard Adams, K.C., who lived to become the County Court Judge of Limerick. On many an afternoon in the Library of the Four Courts in Dublin I have seen a group of barristers surrounding Adams, and listening to a daily budget of quips and cranks and whimsical nonsense which he poured forth to an appreciative audience.

Healy was frequently engaged as counsel with Adams or against him. They were also associated in journalism. I have heard Healy tell a variety of anecdotes of Adams, which may be taken as typical of the word-play of the Munster Circuit.

On one occasion Healy was associated with Adams as counsel for certain defendants who, at a consultation with their counsel, instructed them to turn the trial to account for publicity purposes by insulting the judge, and treating the court with studied disrespect. When their counsel refused to be parties to such a proceeding, the clients angrily left the consultation. As they disappeared Adams fired a parting shot at them: " By God! " he said, " I'd rather defend a menagerie."

*Apropos* of menageries there was a fellow-circuiteer of Adams and Healy—let us call him X.—whose appearance was so suggestive of that of a monkey that he became the frequent object of jests attributing to him the possession of a tail and other simian characistics. At a meeting of the circuit after the long vacation, some of the Bar were describing the route of their return journey from a holiday which a party of them had spent in Germany. It appeared that some had travelled home by car, others by rail, others by river-boat. " I know how X. covered the journey," said Adams. " How?" asked a listener. " Why, of course, he crossed the Black Forest swinging himself from tree to tree."

At one time there was a tendency to reproach Adams with not having subscribed to some political Fund. He waited until somebody had the temerity to taunt him with the absence of his name from the list of subscribers. " You need not trouble about that," was his quick

reply, " the next £50 you see in the list acknow-
ledged from ' Nemo ' will be mine."

In a political libel case Adams was belittling
the plaintiff whom Healy represented.   When
Healy complained that Adams seemed to regard
his client as " an extinct volcano," Adams retorted, " No, it would be flattery to call the
plaintiff an extinct volcano.  He is more like an
extinct fusee."  On another occasion where a
lapse from religious orthodoxy was attributed to
a litigant, and it was said on his behalf that his
opinions had been the same since his earliest
infancy—" In other words," retorted Adams,
" he got baptism and vaccination on the same
day, and neither took."

There was a time when some Irish newspapers were in the habit of reminding their
readers that a small section of Irish M.P.'s, who
only numbered eight, counted " sixteen on a
division " in the House of Commons.   This
phrase, " sixteen on a division " became a
popular catch-phrase of the time.  Adams was
cross-examining a country mayor about his
drinking achievements.  " How many glasses of
whiskey did you drink?" asked Adams.  " Only
four," said the Mayor.  " Only four!" said
Adams, " that's equivalent to eight half-glasses,
isn't it?"  " I suppose so," replied the Mayor."
" Or, in other words, ' sixteen on a division ' in
your stomach?" asked Adams.  The Mayor's
answer was lost in general laughter.

When Adams became County Court Judge of Limerick his court became a popular resort. The cinemas and publichouses were deserted. The people loved good jokes, and they were sure to hear plenty of them when Healy appeared as Counsel before Judge Adams. On one occasion, when Healy was arguing a case, Judge Adams said: " The Court will adjourn for luncheon." As the judge rose he was observed to search his pockets for money, and to exhibit disappointment at finding none. Then he was heard to address Healy: " Mr. Healy, could you be so kind as to lend the Court a bob? "

On another occasion Healy was walking with Adams in one of the back streets of Limerick when they were overtaken by an habitual criminal whom the judge had sentenced more than once to various terms of hard labour. The delinquent was driving an ass's cart with poultry and eggs in it. " God bless you, my lord," said the old lag. " The same to you," said the judge. " and I hope you're not going to throw any of those eggs at me." " God forbid," said the poultryman, " shure there's not a hen in Limerick that could lay an egg to be thrown at your lordship."

I wish I could write down these stories with the crispness and gaiety which gave them point when Healy related them.

Another well-known leader of the Munster

Circuit was a kinsman of Healy's, Denis Baylor
Sullivan, K.C., whose second Christian name
suggested the nickname of "The Biler." I
remember his relating that "The Biler" once
defended a lady who was convicted of some
seditious offence, and sentenced to six months
imprisonment. Her counsel visited her in jail
and tried to console her by the poetic reminder
that "Stone walls do not a prison make, nor
iron bars a cage." "Ah, Mr. Sullivan," was the
matter-of-fact reply, "they make a very good
imitation."

# CHAPTER XIII.

## GRAY'S INN.

# CHAPTER XIII.

## *Gray's Inn.*

TIM HEALY was admitted to the Ancient Society of Gray's Inn as a law student in 1880, when he was a young man of 25. This was at a time when it was part of the curriculum of an Irish law student to keep four terms at one of the English Inns of Court. None of the English Inns of Court have, during the last two centuries, been more frequented by Irish law students, or have extended a more friendly welcome to them than Gray's Inn. Healy became a popular member of the society, joining cordially and sympathetically, whenever a suitable opportunity offered, in its collegiate activities.

In 1910, thirty years after his original admission, he received the particular honour of being elected a Bencher of the Inn, thereby becoming one of its Governing Body, and a colleague of Lords Birkenhead and Merrivale, whom he had known in public life, and of Lord Atkin, who was a native of the County Cork, and became one of Healy's most valued friends.

It was after he became a Bencher of Gray's Inn that my relations with Healy gradually ripened from an agreeable acquaintanceship into an intimate friendship. We had been fellow Benchers of King's Inn in Dublin for many years. When we became fellow Benchers of Gray's Inn, we were doubly allied. We frequently co-operated with each other in taking an interest in the young Irishmen who came to Gray's Inn.

During his Governor-Generalship of the Irish Free State he was entertained by the members of Gray's Inn at a banquet, which was rendered memorable by speeches by Lord Birkenhead and Lord Merrivale in honour of the guest of the evening, and by a delightful speech from Healy himself in acknowledging the enthusiasm with which the whole society united to do him honour.

At last in 1929 he was elected to the highest office in the gift of the society—that of Treasurer—and in that year he presided over the meetings of the society with conspicuous dignity and success.

Healy was beloved by his colleagues at Gray's Inn, who soon discovered that he could lay aside every trace of polemical fierceness among his friends, and that " Tiger Tim " could display, in the sphere of social intercourse, the disposition and temperament of a warm-hearted child.

Healy's affection for the society was reflected in an article which he contributed to *Graya,* the collegiate magazine of Gray's Inn, giving some recollections of the Inn during his fifty years' membership. From this article the following passages are extracted. The author apologises for not omitting a kindly reference to himself.

When I joined the Inn it was a great enjoyment to youngsters like myself to dine in the students' messes, but at that time Gray's Inn, which is now probably the most opulent and attractive of the four Inns of Court, was in low water. The fact that this Inn for centuries had been the favourite one to which Irish students resorted, made us the more loyal in our allegiance to it in its days of depression and adversity. In those days, when the Benchers left the dining-hall, the students were more frolicsome than they seem to-day. Once, to content them, I had to sing a rebel Irish song, and afterwards, when John Redmond, M.P., joined the Inn I think he did the same, for there is a tradition that Lord Merrivale, now President of the Probate, Divorce, and Admiralty Division, was rebuked by the Bench for not checking more sternly the vivacity of his juniors. Redmond, I think, was docked a term on the unfounded allegation that he refused to drink the Queen's health in 1881. What struck me most was the kindliness and comradeship of the other students towards us, despite the fact that we were waging in Parliament a very unrelenting conflict with the Government of the day as regards Ireland.

Later on, if I may skip over thirty years, I should like to chronicle that when I was elected a Bencher of Gray's Inn in 1910, nothing impressed me more than the constant paternal kindness of the Benchers towards Indian students. At one time the Indian students joined Gray's Inn in such numbers that, on the day I was called in 1903 a witty Oxford man, in replying to the toast of his health, said " Kipling remarks, ' You can hear the East *a-callin'*, but you must come to Gray's Inn Hall to see them *called.*"

Gray's Inn has produced many distinguished men as lawyers, orators and parliamentarians. Without being invidious, I should class as foremost amongst them Lord Merrivale and Lord Birkenhead.

I was a student with Lord Merrivale, who told me he had often, in the reporters' gallery of the House of Commons, taken down my speeches. His uprise to dignity and eminence should be an incentive to every student, and should dispel the doleful impression that without favouritism, nepotism or backing, no unknown youth can make headway.

The career of Lord Birkenhead affords similar inspiration. President of the Oxford Union as a youth, he strolled into the House of Commons sure-footedly, and his maiden speech proclaimed him an unrivalled orator. In the House of Lords as Lord Chancellor his judgments from the Woolsack, as well as his political addresses, led a peer of opposite politics to exclaim to me: " He holds the House in the hollow of his hand." In olden days men sought out patrons to forward their advance judicially or politically. Lord Merrivale and Lord Birkenhead cared for none of these things.

A further outstanding personality in Gray's Inn is Sir Plunket Barton. A former law officer and judge in Ireland, he acts to-day as a sort of liaison between English and Irish members of Bench and Bar. None of us knows so much as he about the history and associations of the Inn, and we all read with great interest his contributions to *Graya,* from each one of which we learn something about the great figures that flourished here in past times.

At the present day it is pleasing to record that, with financial prosperity which enables scholarships and exhibitions to be multiplied, Gray's Inn stands foremost, or almost foremost in pride of place among the Inns of Court. Sir John Holker's bequest of £100,000 enabled the library to be greatly enlarged and beautified, and the skilful stewardship of that shrewd economist and financier, Sir Miles Mattinson, K.C., led to reforms which of themselves set the Inn firmly on its feet.

As for my Treasurership, the honour of being selected by such colleagues led me to undertake an office which I would fain have declined. Some spark of vanity, however, is latent in the most elderly, and when I preside at a Pension in Gray's Inn, the humble student of 1880 is not without a touch of pride at holding the position which has crowned his forensic career.

Many good stories were told about Tim Healy at Gray's Inn. I remember a conversation between him and Lord Ashbourne, Lord Chancellor of Ireland, who was also a Bencher of the Society. It happened one day at the Benchers' luncheon table in the ancient hall of that society. It was soon after the publication of Tim Healy's book, *Stolen Waters*. "I've just read your book, Tim," said Lord Ashbourne. "I can't believe that," said Healy. "Well, I've read part of it at all events," said Ashbourne. "Oh yes," said Healy, "I quite understand, you looked up the letter ' A ' in the index."

# CHAPTER XIV.

## THE LAST PHASE.

# CHAPTER XIV.

## *The Last Phase.*

FOUR years after Tim Healy's retirement from Parliament, in 1922, the question of the selection of a suitable Governor-General for the recently created Irish Free State came up for settlement. A new chapter in the history of the relations between Great Britain and Ireland had been initiated, and the situation was a delicate one. What was wanted was a man of courage and capacity upon whose conscientious discharge of the duties of a difficult post both Great Britain and Ireland could confidently rely. When Tim Healy's appointment was announced the fitness of the appointment was almost universally recognised.

During the term of his Governor-Generalship I had the honour of being his guest at the Viceregal Lodge in Dublin. Around the table were gathered several representative Irishmen and several members of his family. He was a charming host. His bearing was dignified and simple. His greeting was unaffected and hospitable. Never can His Majesty have been represented in Ireland by a more gracious deputy. He had once been described as " the stormiest petrel and the most unquiet spirit of

his time." It was obvious that the petrel had
ceased to revel in the storm, and that the
unquiet spirit had found rest. He seemed to be
absorbed in charitable activities and in dis-
charging the duties of his office under the new
Irish Constitution. Towards the end of his life
Tim Healy mellowed and softened. The only
visible vestiges of the fire and fierceness of
former days were their embers which were
reflected fitfully in the corners of his expressive
eyes, and were sometimes fanned to a flame by
memories of past conflicts or by day-dreams
of a happier Ireland.

Tim Healy's brilliancy in conversation was
comparable to that of a celebrated namesake
of his—Father James Healy, who was for
many years the parish priest of Little Bray, in
County Wicklow. It is a strange coincidence
that two of the most famously witty Irishmen
of our time have borne the same surname.
Yet, they were not related to each other.
Perhaps the explanation may be that "ready
wit" was a characteristic trait of the clan to
which they both belonged. Both of them were
intimate friends of mine at different times of
my life. I never met them together, but I have
a clear recollection of the difference between
the brilliance of the two men. It was like the
difference between summer sunshine and
forked lightning. There never was anything
mordant about Father Healy. His conversation

always seemed to sparkle radiantly. Tim Healy was no less sparkling, but was at his best when some compelling forces from within or from without roused him to flare up and flash electrically. As he mellowed in later life, he reminded me more and more of his lovable namesake.

Tim Healy always took a patriotic interest in Irish antiquities and in Irish history and topography. The following glimpse of this side of him came to the author from a friend and comrade of his who recalled a walk with him in the hills overlooking the beautiful bay of Glengariff. It was at the time when Healy was a combative politician. The glamour, the mystery, and the silence of the scene moved Healy to a characteristic outburst of patriotic emotion. He turned to his companion and exclaimed: " Look at that perfect panorama of peace and beauty. It's ours! It's ours! It's Ireland! 'Tis worth fighting for."

Tim Healy was fortunate in his wife and family. They were devoted to him, and he to them. Of his three daughters the eldest was his loving companion who consoled and comforted him after the death of his wife, and helped him in the social side of his life as Governor-General. His second daughter became the wife of Mr. Justice Timothy Sullivan, a distinguished lawyer, who now fills the high position of President of the High Court of the

Irish Free State. His third daughter became a nun. His eldest son, Joe, followed his father to the Irish Bar, served in the war in the naval division, and fought with distinction at Gallipoli. His second son, Paul, became a Jesuit priest, and a notable scholar and preacher. His third son adopted the medical profession, and became the Master of one of the principal hospitals of Dublin.

The member of his family who was most closely associated with him in the public eye was his brother Maurice, whose son (also named Maurice) is now a promising young K.C. of the English Bar. The elder Maurice Healy was in manner and temperament more retiring and unobtrusive than his brother Tim. His intellectual gifts were outstanding, and he made his mark as one of the leading solicitors of the south of Ireland, and as a useful member of parliament. An intimate friend of the Healy family informed me that Tim was a very young child when his mother died in childbirth, at the coming into the world of Maurice. A nurse who was deeply attached to the family carried the baby into the nursery and, placing it in Tim's arms, said to the child, " This little boy has no mother now, and you will have to be a mother to him." Tim held the infant for a moment and said he would. Although he could not have understood the significance of the scene, his subsequent actions did not belie his promise.

The brothers were very close friends and comrades, and wrote to each other almost every day of their lives. Maurice's solid commonsense sometimes acted as a corrective to Tim's exuberant impetuosity both in Parliament and in the courts. It was when Tim was Governor-General of the Irish Free State that a telegram called him to his dying brother's bedside. He travelled to Cork, but arrived too late. Maurice had passed away. One of the family described to me how Tim fell on his knees beside the body, sobbing and moaning, "Oh, Maurice! Maurice!" The loss of Maurice left him lonely and forlorn.

The amiable side of Healy's personality was very well expressed in the following passage from the obituary notice which was published in the *Times,* in March, 1931. " In private life Healy was one of the most kindhearted and lovable of men. The manysided charm of his nature—his ready wit, his varied experience in politics and his fine appreciation of literature made him a delightful companion and a welcome guest of distinguished society."

Among the elements which rendered Healy's character so interesting to his contemporaries were the contrasts which it so often exhibited. He had at his command equally inexhaustible stores of vitriolic invective and of the milk of human kindness, of rhetorical ruthlessness and of tenderness of heart. Similar contrasts were exhibited in his life-story, with its beginning as a shorthand clerk, its series of tempestuous adventures in public life, and its peaceful culmination in the Viceregal Lodge.

Besides these contrasts, which lent a special picturesqueness to his personality, he impressed his contemporaries by the possession of certain qualities of mind and heart which won the affection and respect of a wide circle. Conspicuous among these qualities were his disinterestedness, his physical and moral courage, his fidelity in friendship, his dependability in all his personal relations, a dignity of mind which had its sure foundation in religion, and an unfailing sense of public duty.

Here let us say good-bye to Tim Healy. In the course of a strenuous career his combative temperament aroused many animosities, and challenged a great deal of criticism. But enough had been said to show that there was another side to the picture, and to explain why a large circle of personal friends cherish an affectionate recollection of his brilliant mind, his brave spirit and his kind heart.

INDEX.

# INDEX.

Adams, Richard, K.C., the witty County Court Judge of Limerick, 99-102

Advocacy, Healy's methods of, 83, 84

America, gift of a hat to Healy from, 62, 63

Antiquities and History, Healy's interest in, 7, 117

Appreciation of political opponents, Healy's generous, 79, 80

Ashbourne Lord, Lord Chancellor of Ireland, offers Healy his "silk gown" at the Irish Bar; a colleague of Healy as Bencher of Gray's Inn; his compliment to Healy about his book, and Healy's reply, 87, 112

Atkin Lord, Lord of Appeal, belonged to a County Cork family; a colleague of Healy as a Bencher of Gray's Inn; their friendship, 107

Atkinson, John, K.C., Attorney-General for Ireland, and Lord of Appeal, a fellow-member with Healy of the Munster Circuit, 99

"At sea," the judge who never was, 93

"Babe in the Wood," The, 93

Balfour, The Right Honourable Arthur James, M.P., 59-61, 75.

Balfour, The Right Honourable Gerald, M.P., 75, 76

Bantry, Healy's birthplace, 11, 22

Bar, the Irish, 80-103

Beaverbrook, Lord, his pen portrait of Healy as a parliamentarian, 53, 54

Bernal Osborne, 91

Big Game Hunting, 70

Biggar, Joseph, M.P., Healy's tutor and co-operator in Parliamentary obstruction, 27-31

Birkenhead, the Earl of, his maiden speech; he describes Healy, and Healy describes him; they are colleagues as Benchers of Gray's Inn, 45, 46, 77-79, 107, 108, 111

Birrell, Right Honourable Augustine, M.P., 70

"Bivouac of the Dead," 78

Blackwater, the River, Healy's boyhood on the banks of, 11

"Bob," Healy lends the Court a, 102

British statesmen, Healy's judgments upon, 63-80

"Buccaneer in broadcloth," Healy described as the "beau ideal" of a, 55

Burke, Edmund, Lord Birkenhead's reference to, 46
Butt, K.C., Isaac, Healy's meeting with; Butt's remarkable argument in a Contempt of Court case, 14, 15, 19

Campbell, The Right Honourable James, *see* Glenavy
Campbell-Bannerman, The Right Honourable Sir Henry, M.P., 47
Carson, Right Honourable Sir Edward, afterwards Lord of Appeal, 79
Catholic Schools, Healy's remarkable speech about Education in, 61, 62
Cavendishes, the neighbourly relations between the Healys and the, 11, 12
Chance, Sir Arthur, 31
Chamberlain, the Right Honourable Joseph, M.P., 70-72
Character, some of the elements in Healy's, 119, 120
Christian Brothers' School, Healy's education at a, 13
Cork, Healy a native of West, 11
"Collusive Block," the, a Parliamentary device of Healy's, 51
Constructive legislation, Healy's contributions to, 52
Curzon of Kedleston, Lord, 29

Davitt, Michael, M.P., 23
Devonshire, the Duke of, 11, 12
Disinterestedness, Healy's, 62, 120
Don Quixote, Healy compared to, 43
Dowse, Baron, witty Irish judge; his reply in the House of Commons to Bernal Osborne; Healy's reply to a question from him, 91, 92
Duke, Sir Henry, *see* Merrivale.
"Duodecimo Demosthenes," the, 47

Electioneering experiences, 39

FitzGerald, Lord Edward, 76
"Fusee," the extinct, 101

"Gamin of Genius," a, 51
Gesture, a characteristic, 84, 85
Gladstone, the Right Honourable, W. E., M.P., 67, 68, 76
Glenavy, Lord, Lord Chancellor of Ireland, Healy's witty reference to, 93, 94
Glengariff, Healy's walk and interesting talk at, 117

Gray's Inn. Healy becomes successively, Student, Barrister, Bencher, and Treasurer at, 7, 83, 107-112
*Graya,* Healy's article contributed to, 109-112
Governor-General of the Irish Free State, Healy becomes, 115, 116
Grosvenor, the Countess, wife of George Wyndham, 76

Harcourt, Right Honourable, Sir William, M.P., 30
Healy, the Rev. Father James, Timothy Healy compared with, 116, 117
Healy, Timothy, his wife and children, 117, 118
Healy, Timothy, his father, 11, 12
Healy, Maurice, Timothy Healy's brother, 84, 118, 119
Healy, Maurice, K.C., Timothy Healy's nephew, 13, 118
"Healy clause," the, 52, 53
"Heliopolis," George Wyndham's name for Healy's residence, 77
Hen, a discriminating, 102
Hicks-Beach, Sir Michael, 79, 80
Holker, Sir John, 112
House of Commons, how Healy was successful in enchaining the attention the, 47
"Horses" and "Asses," question about the transport to South Africa of, 71
"Hunted Hind," Healy's metaphor of the, 46

"Impish Juvenality," Healy's air of, 51
Imprisonments, Timothy Healy's two, 22, 23
Irish Statutes, Healy's intimate familiarity with the modern, 84
Irony and pathos, Healy's power of, 59-62
Ishmael, Healy becomes a political, 39

Jekyll-Hyde duality, Healy's, 51
Journalistic adventures, some of Timothy Healy's, 39

Kettle, A. J., Healy's electioneering encounter with, 39, 40
Kipling, Rudyard, quotation from, 110
King's Inn, Dublin, Healy a Bencher of, 83

Lecky, the Right Honourable W. E., M.P., caught napping by Healy, 54, 55
Lismore, the home-place of the Healy family, 11, 12, 13
Libel action, Healy's successful, 85

Lloyd George, Right Honourable David, M.P., 69, 70
Long, Right Honourable Walter, M.P., afterwards Viscount Long, 79, 80
Londonderry South, Healy once M.P. for, 24
Longford, North, Healy once M.P., for, 24
Loreburn, Lord, Lord Chancellor of Great Britain, 87
Louth, North, Healy once M.P., for, 24
Lucy, Sir Henry, 45

McNeill, J. S. Swift, K.C., M.P., 37
Mattinson, K.C., Sir Miles, 112
" Menagerie," the, 100
Merrivale, Lord, 79, 107, 108, 109
Modesty of mind, Healy's, 81, 84
Morley, Right Honble. John, M.P., 68, 69
Monaghan, County of, Healy once M.P. for, 23
" Moses and the Rock," the Miracle of, 94
Munster Circuit, the, 99-103

Napoleon, Healy compared to, 44, 45
*Nation,* the *Irish,* Healy once Parliamentary correspondent to, 19
Newcastle on Tyne, Healy once a railway shorthand clerk at, 13, 15, 19

O'Brien, Peter (afterwards Lord O'Brien, Lord Chief Justice of Ireland, 23, 80, 92, 99
Obstructionist, Healy as a Parliamentary, 27-31
O'Connor, T. P., M.P., 37, 38
O'Hara, Theodore, 79
O'Leary, John, 27

Palles, The Right Honourable Christopher, Lord Chief Baron in Ireland, 12
Parnell, M.P., Charles Stewart, 19, 20, 21, 27, 35-38, 43, 86
Parliament, Healy's reasons for retiring from, 63
" Parliamentarian," A great, 53, 54
Parties, Healy's attitude towards British, " A plague upon both your houses," 75
Paul Jones, Healy compared to, 43
" Peter Pan," " A parliamentary," 51
" Petty Pontius Pilates," Healy's description of a Parliamentary group, 72
Pitman, Isaac, 13
Pope, Alexander, Healy quotes a couplet from, 30

Poultryman, story of Judge Adams and the Limerick, 102

*Punch* cartoon of Healy, 76

Quixote, Healy compared to, 43
Quinn, Thomas, M.P., 47

Redmond, John, M.P., 37, 109
Redmond, William, M.P., 37
Reid, Sir Robert, *see* Loreburn
Rosebery, Earl of, 70
Ross, The Right Honourable Sir John, last Lord Chancellor of Ireland, 93
Runciman, The Right Honourable Walter, M.P., 46
Rupert, Healy compared to Prince, 43

St. Aldwyn, Viscount, *see* Hicks-Beach.
" Second Calling," Healy's witty allusion to a, 92, 93
Shillelagh, Healy in self-defence draws his, 40
" Silk gowns," Healy's two, 87
" Sixteen on a division," Judge Adams' allusion to, 101
Speaker, A veiled attack upon the, 27-29
Speeches of Timothy Healy, Two remarkable, 59-63
" Stone walls do not a prison make," 103
" Strange and solitary enigma," A, 44
Sullivan, A. M., M.P., Timothy Healy's uncle, 12, 13, 15
Sullivan, Denis Baylor, K.C., Timothy Healy's uncle, 103
Sullivan, Mr. Serjeant, K.C., Timothy Healy's cousin, 13, 15
Sullivan, Mr. Justice, Timothy Healy's son-in-law, 117
Sullivan, T. D., M.P., 12
*Sunday Express*, The, 53
Swift, Healy compared to Dean, 43
" Swinging from tree to tree," Judge Adam's description of a fellow circuiteer, 100

Tactics, Healy described by Mr. Lecky as a master of " two o'clock in the morning," 54, 55
Tactics, Healy described by Lord Beaverbrook as a master of " red herring," 55
" Tiger Tim's Parliamentary tactics, 51-55, 108
*Times,* Obituary notice of Healy in the, 119
Treasurer of Gray's Inn, Healy elected to be, 108
Turkish prayers, Gladstone and Healy discuss, 68

" Uganda " speech the, an example of Healy's ironical style, 59-61

" Uncle Tim's Cabin," a nickname of Viceregal Lodge, 77

Viceregal Lodge, Healy at the, 77, 115, 116
Viceroy's invitation, Healy's reason for refusing a, 46
Voice, the charm of Healy's, 47

Walker, The Right Honourable Sir Samuel, Lord Chancellor of Ireland, 85
Water, Healy's " only " glass of, 85, 86
Wexford, County, Healy once M.P. for, 22
Wilson, P. W., of the *Daily News* and *Pearson's Magazine,* 44, 45
Wyndham, The Right Honourable George, M.P., 76, 77

" Yashmak " Breach of Promise case, the, 94, 95